ENERGY IN SONG TAROT

Guidebook

ELIZABETH RODRIGUEZ

Copyright © 2025

by Elizabeth Rodriguez

All Rights Reserved.

Published in the United States by

R-Squared Publishing, LLC.

Book and Cover designed by Elizabeth Rodriguez

First Edition

Disclaimer

Intellectual Property Notice

The *Energy in Song Tarot* Guidebook and deck are an original work of art and creative interpretation inspired by the energy, themes, and cultural impact of various songs and musical movements.

All song titles and performer names referenced throughout this deck are used purely for descriptive purposes as inspiration to evoke the mood associated with the song.

- These titles and names are the property of their respective copyright and trademark owners.
- This product and its creator are not affiliated with, endorsed by, or sponsored by any of the named artists, estates, record labels, or publishers.

No Endorsement Intended

The inclusion of song titles and performer names:

- Does not imply endorsement, partnership, or sponsorship by the referenced musicians or their representatives.
- Is solely intended to acknowledge cultural influences and provide thematic connections for symbolic interpretation within the tarot tradition.

Copyright & Licensing

The artwork, design, and written content of the *Energy in Song Tarot* deck are wholly original and owned by the creator of the *Energy in Song Tarot* deck.

Lyrics, melodies, and musical compositions are not reproduced within this deck.

Any resemblance to real lyrics, likenesses, or protected works is purely coincidental and unintentional.

For Entertainment Use

The *Energy in Song Tarot* is created for:
- Personal insight, spiritual exploration, and creative storytelling.
- It is not intended for fortune-telling, legal, medical, or financial advice.
- Use of this deck is at your own discretion.

Limitation of Liability

By using the *Energy in Song Tarot* deck, you agree that the creator and distributors:
- Are not liable for any interpretations, decisions, or actions taken based on the use of these cards.
- Make no guarantees regarding outcomes or results related to readings or interpretations.

TABLE OF CONTENTS

Welcome to Energy in Song Tarot 1

Use of Tarot 2

The Soul's Journey 2

Using Astrological Attributes and Elements 4

Major Arcana 8

Minor Arcana 21

    Wands 24

    Cups 32

    Swords 40

    Pentacles 48

Type of Card Spreads and When to Use Them 55

    Choosing the Right Spread 55

    Common Single, Two, and Three Card Spreads 56

    Common Three, Four, and Five Card Spreads 57

    Common Five, Seven, and Nine Card Spreads 58

    Celtic Cross Spread (Classic and Comprehensive) 59

    Position of Classic Celtic Cross Spread 59

    Specialty and Spiritual Spreads 60

Interpreting Timing in Tarot 61

Reading The Cards 63

    Using the 3-Card Spread 63

    Using the 7-Card Spread 64

    Tips for Effective Readings 64

Author's Note 65

ENERGY IN SONG

TAROT

Guidebook

Welcome to Energy in Song Tarot

The *Energy in Song Tarot Guidebook* offers a unique way to understand energy movement. The Major Arcana becomes a playlist of life's biggest themes like spiritual awakening, love, loss, growth, and purpose. The Minor Arcana suits become genres and moods representing everyday experiences.

As you experience the Minor Arcana, each suit has an energy theme that fits with the suit element. For example, the Wands represent the element of fire. The wands suit focuses on passion, drive, and creativity. The card images and songs are meant to feel up-tempo with motivating songs about ambition and desire.

The Cups represent the element of water. The cups suit focuses on emotions, love, and relationships. The card images and songs are meant to feel soulful with romantic ballads and heart break anthems.

The Swords represent the element of air. The swords suit focuses on conflict, truth, and intellect. The card images and songs are meant to illicit self-reflection with story-driven songs about struggle and clarity.

Finally, the Pentacles represent the element of earth. The pentacles suit focuses on work, stability, and growth. The card images and songs are meant to feel earthy with songs about money, hustle, family, and legacy.

The *Energy in Song Tarot* reads like a full album as it moves through life's different emotional and energetic frequencies. It's a powerful tool for clarifying energy because it engages the mind, heart, and spirit simultaneously as you see the patterns of the cards and evoke the feeling and emotion of the songs to make it easier to integrate the energy into your life.

Tarot is a song your soul sings. So, when you read the cards, feel the energy.

Use of Tarot

Tarot can be used by anyone, enthusiasts, energy readers, and intuitive people. Tarot is a tool energy readers use to help clarify the energies they are intuitively receiving. The decks can be used for readings and as tools for storytelling, meditation, and personal development.

The Soul's Journey

Tarot symbolizes the evolution of the consciousness. Where the Fool's Journey is the soul's incarnation, moving from innocence to experience through trials and shadows, and finally to spiritual mastery. Each Major Arcana card represents a step towards greater awareness.

- The Call to Adventure phase starts the journey and represents Innocence and Beginning. It's represented by the Major Arcana cards 0 through 4: The Fool, The Magician, The High Priestess, The Empress, and The Emperor. This phase represents the "ordinary world" before challenges arise. The human being forms their identity, learns about power and structure, and begins to awaken to deeper truths.

- The Initiation phase confronts us with Challenges, Tests, and Transformation. This phase is represented by the Major Arcana cards 5 through 11: The Hierophant, The Lovers, The Chariot, Strength, The Hermit, The Wheel of Fortune, and Justice. Here the traveler leaves the comfort behind and encounters trials. These trials represent the inner and outer struggles that shape one's destiny. This stage reflects adolescence and adulthood and helps to understand the forces of fate and our choices.

- The Abyss phase leads us to explore Death, Rebirth, and the Dark Night of the Soul. This phase is represented by the Major Arcana cards 12 through 16: The Hanged Man, Death, Temperance, The Devil, and The Tower. Here the traveler faces death of the ego, the deepest shadow work, and ultimately transformation. It's the crucible of the soul, where the old self dies so the true self can emerge. This is the most painful and transformative part of life where major crises, spiritual trials, and the collapse of illusions are experienced.

- The Revelations phase helps us to come to terms with the Awakening and Higher Consciousness. This phase is represented by the Major Arcana cards 17 through 20: The Star, The Moon, The Sun, and Judgement. After the fall comes clarity, spiritual awakening, and realization of true purpose. The traveler begins to transcend the material world and unite with higher truths. This phase represents spiritual maturity and integration of the shadow and light within the self.

- The Return phase guides us to integrate the journey, experience, and lessons together in Mastery and Wholeness. This is represented by Major Arcana card 21, The World. The journey ends where it began, but the traveler is forever changed. This is the stage of wholeness and cosmic unity. The soul evolves through cycles, returning to life with wisdom, ready to begin again on a higher spiral.

The Tarots Fool's Journey symbolizes the soul's incarnation as it moves from innocence to experience through trials, shadows, and finally to spiritual mastery. The journey parallels the psychological journey of individualism, the mystical path of enlightenment found in may traditions, and the hero's journey that are told in myths and stories throughout all cultures.

Using Astrological Attributes and Elements

When reading tarot, being familiar with the attributes of the planetary alignment, astrological signs (or Zodiac signs), and the elements helps in creating a bigger picture of the story that the cards are portraying.

The planetary attributes represent the universal forces and archetypes that influence the path and all of the Zodiac signs. The Zodiac signs express personal development and inner growth. Being familiar with the positive negative attributes of each of the star signs as it the relates to the card adds a dimension of personal growth to the reading. The elements reflect the balance of forces in spiritual growth.

Detailed below is a list of the planets for the Major Arcana and their energetic keywords and attributes:

Core Energy Keywords of Planets

Planet	Major Arcana	Core Energy
Uranus	The Fool (0)	Revolution, freedom, innovation
Mercury	The Magician (I)	Communication, intellect, adaptability
Moon	The High Priestess (II)	Intuition, mystery, divine feminine
Venus	The Empress (III)	Love, beauty, fertility
Jupiter	Wheel of Fortune (X)	Expansion, luck, destiny
Neptune	The Hanged Man (XII)	Surrender, spiritual enlightenment
Mars	The Tower (XVI)	Destruction, war, action, sudden events
Sun	The Sun (XIX)	Joy, vitality, radiance
Pluto	Judgment (XX)	Death, rebirth, transformation
Saturn	The World (XXI)	Structure, completion, mastery

Detailed below is a list of Zodiac signs for the Major Arcana and their energetic keywords and attributes:

Core Energy Keywords of Zodiac Signs		
Zodiac Sign	Major Arcana	Core Energy
Aries (♈)	The Emperor (IV)	Leadership, new beginnings, action
Taurus (♉)	The Hierophant (V)	Stability, values, traditions
Gemini (♊)	The Lovers (VI)	Duality, communication, choice
Cancer (♋)	The Chariot (VII)	Emotional resilience, willpower
Leo (♌)	Strength (VIII)	Courage, vitality, heart-centered action
Virgo (♍)	The Hermit (IX)	Wisdom, service, self-reflection
Libra (♎)	Justice (XI)	Balance, relationships, fairness
Scorpio (♏)	Death (XIII)	Transformation, endings, deep power
Sagittarius (♐)	Temperance (XIV)	Expansion, harmony, higher wisdom
Capricorn (♑)	The Devil (XV)	Ambition, mastery, overcoming limitation
Aquarius (♒)	The Star (XVII)	Hope, universal consciousness
Pisces (♓)	The Moon (XVIII)	Illusion, dreams, spiritual surrender

Detailed below is a list of the elements, Major Arcana alignment, and their keyword meaning:

Core Energy Keywords of the Elements		
Element	**Major Arcana**	**Core Energy**
Fire (▲)	The Emperor (IV), Strength (VIII), Wheel of Fortune (X), Temperance (XIV), The Tower (XVI), The Sun (XIX), Judgment (XX)	Spirit, Action
Water (▼)	The High Priestess (II), The Chariot (VII), The Hanged Man (XII), Death (XIII), The Moon (XVIII)	Emotions, Intuition
Air (▲)	The Fool (0), The Magician (I), The Lovers (VI), Justice (XI), The Star (XVII)	Mind, Intellect
Earth (▼)	The Empress (III), The Hierophant (V), The Hermit (IX), The Devil (XV), The World (XXI)	Material, Stability

MAJOR ARCANA

Major Arcana

The Major Arcana are depicted with 22 cards starting with the unnumbered or zero card (The Fool). As stated in the previous section, when reading the Major Arcana sequentially, the Tarot outlines the stages of growth, transformation, and awakening that everyone encounters in the human experience of life. So, if we also see tarot as a tool that guides us through the evolution of our consciousness, we can begin to learn about power and structure, and start to awaken to our deeper truths.

We can begin to reflect on our relationships, challenges, and inner growth from our adolescence and into adulthood with an understanding of the forces and energies at play. As we move through the cards, we also begin to understand with the hopes and strength to overcome the painful and transformative parts of life like major crises, spiritual trials, and the collapse of illusions. As we step through to the end of the 22 Major Arcana, the idea is to become spiritually mature and build upon all the identities and lessons as we integrate them to be a more whole and balanced being.

As you use this tarot deck, a list of keywords and phrases have been provided to get an initial understanding of the energy each card is reflecting. Keywords have been listed to define the upright and reversed meaning of the card. If you use the cards for personal development, soul journey, or just the human experience, keywords are listed for those areas as well.

In the end, become comfortable and familiar with your cards. Become comfortable and familiar with how you are being led to interpret the cards, images, song titles, lyrics, and placement of cards.

Go with the flow of energy and have fun.

THE FOOL
Card number: 0 *or unnumbered*
Astrological Ruler and Element: Uranus and Air
Song Inspiration: "Don't Stop Believin"
Symbolism through Song and Keywords: New beginnings, faith, and the courage to leap into the unknown. Sudden change, freedom, originality, breaking boundaries
Core Energy: Revolution, freedom, innovation
Meaning: New beginnings, innocence, taking a leap of faith, trusting the journey.
Reverse Meaning: Fear of change, reckless choices, hesitation, missed opportunities
Soul's Journey: The call to adventure.
Human Experience: Birth of the self, trust in life, stepping into the unknown

THE MAGICIAN
Card number: I
Astrological Ruler and Element: Mercury and Air
Song Inspiration: "The Man in The Mirror"
Symbolism through Song and Keywords: Transformation through self-awareness and inner power. Manifestation, willpower, tools for the journey, communication, intellect, skill, adaptability
Core Energy: Communication, intellect, adaptability
Meaning: Manifestation, skill, focused willpower, using resources wisely
Reverse Meaning: Manipulation, misuse of power, lack of focus, untapped potential.
Soul's Journey: Meeting the Mentor (inner guide)
Human Experience: Realizing you have the power to create your reality

THE HIGH PRIESTESS
Card number: II
Astrological Ruler and Element: Moon and Water
Song Inspiration: "Superstition"
Symbolism through Song and Keywords: Intuition, hidden knowledge, mystery, subconscious
Core Energy: Intuition, mystery, divine feminine
Meaning: Intuition, inner wisdom, mysteries revealed, spiritual insight
Reverse Meaning: Secrets, blocked intuition, denial of truth, inner disconnect
Soul's Journey: Crossing the threshold into mystery
Human Experience: Developing inner wisdom, accessing subconscious truths

THE EMPRESS
Card number: III
Astrological Ruler and Element: Venus and Earth
Song Inspiration: "Isn't She Lovely"
Symbolism through Song and Keywords: Creation and the beauty of life. Nurturing, abundance, creativity, love, beauty, fertility
Core Energy: Love, beauty, fertility
Meaning: Fertility, creativity, nurturing, abundance, harmony with nature
Reverse Meaning: Creative blocks, dependence, neglect, smothering relationships
Soul's Journey: Receiving gifts/allies
Human Experience: Experiencing love, safety, and growth through nature and relationships

THE EMPEROR
Card number: IV
Astrological Ruler and Element: Aries and Fire
Song Inspiration: "My Way"
Symbolism through Song and Keywords: Structure, discipline, order, authority, leadership, initiative, self-mastery
Core Energy: Leadership, new beginnings, action
Meaning: Structure, authority, discipline, leadership, stability
Reverse Meaning: Rigidity, domination, lack of control, misuse of authority.
Soul's Journey: Establishing the known world
Human Experience: Learning boundaries, rules, and worldly systems

THE HIERPHANT
Card number: V
Astrological Ruler and Element: Taurus and Earth
Song Inspiration: "Respect"
Symbolism through Song and Keywords: Tradition, community, guidance, spiritual authority, values
Core Energy: Stability, values, traditions
Meaning: Tradition, spiritual guidance, community, higher learning
Reverse Meaning: Rebellion, questioning authority, breaking free from dogma
Soul's Journey: Finding the path or teacher
Human Experience: Seeking meaning through belief systems or mentors

THE LOVERS
Card number: VI
Astrological Ruler and Element: Gemini and Air
Song Inspiration: "Endless Love"
Symbolism through Song and Keywords: Choice, duality, relationships, union, harmony, meaningful connection
Core Energy: Duality, communication, choice
Meaning: Deep connection, harmony, relationships, major choices, alignment
Reverse Meaning: Disharmony, imbalance, unhealthy relationships, misaligned choices
Soul's Journey: Facing temptation, inner conflict
Human Experience: Learning balance between desire, duty, and alignment with true self

THE CHARIOT
Card number: VII
Astrological Ruler and Element: Cancer and Water
Song Inspiration: "Ain't No Stoppin' Us Now"
Symbolism through Song and Keywords: Victory through determination and willpower. Control and emotional mastery
Core Energy: Emotional resilience, willpower
Meaning: Determination, control, willpower, overcoming challenges
Reverse Meaning: Lack of direction, scattered energy, loss of control.
Soul's Journey: Test of strength and resolve
Human Experience: Asserting independence, mastering conflicting forces

STRENGTH
Card number: VIII
Astrological Ruler and Element: Leo and Fire
Song Inspiration: "I Will Survive"
Symbolism through Song and Keywords: Inner courage, resilience, compassion, self-mastery, heart energy, vitality
Core Energy: Courage, vitality, heart-centered action
Meaning: Inner strength, courage, compassion, mastering instincts.
Reverse Meaning: Fear, self-doubt, weakness, inability to face challenges
Soul's Journey: Facing the first great trail
Human Experience: Balancing raw emotion and higher consciousness

THE HERMIT
Card number: IX
Astrological Ruler and Element: Virgo and Earth
Song Inspiration: "Alone Again (Naturally)"
Symbolism through Song and Keywords: Reflection, solitude, and seeking inner truth. Introspection, inner guidance, wisdom, service, analysis
Core Energy: Wisdom, service, self-reflection
Meaning: Soul searching, inner guidance, introspection, spiritual growth
Reverse Meaning: Isolation, loneliness, avoidance, refusing to look within
Soul's Journey: Retreat and reflection
Human Experience: Searching inward for spiritual truth and self-discovery

WHEEL OF FORTUNE
Card number: X
Astrological Ruler and Element: Jupiter and Fire
Song Inspiration: "What Goes Around…Comes Around"
Symbolism through Song and Keywords: Cycles, fate, changes, expansion, destiny, growth, luck
Core Energy: Expansion, luck, destiny
Meaning: Positive change, destiny, luck, cycles turning in your favor
Reverse Meaning: Setbacks, resistance to change, bad luck, stuck in a cycle.
Soul's Journey: Turning point, destiny revealed
Human Experience: Recognizing life's ups and downs, learning acceptance

JUSTICE
Card number: XI
Astrological Ruler and Element: Libra and Air
Song Inspiration: "What's Going On"
Symbolism through Song and Keywords: Truth, accountability, karma, balance, fairness, law, higher moral alignment
Core Energy: Balance, relationships, fairness
Meaning: Truth, fairness, balance, accountability, karmic consequences.
Reverse Meaning: Dishonesty, bias, lack of accountability, unfairness
Soul's Journey: Facing consequences
Human Experience: Understanding cause and effect, aligning with integrity

THE HANGED MAN
Card number: XII
Astrological Ruler and Element: Neptune and Water
Song Inspiration: "Let it Be"
Symbolism through Song and Keywords: Surrender, new perspective, sacrifice, spiritual vision, transcendence
Core Energy: Surrender, spiritual enlightenment
Meaning: Surrender, new perspective, letting go, spiritual insight
Reverse Meaning: Stalling, victimhood, refusal to release control, missed enlightenment
Soul's Journey: Letting go, seeing differently
Human Experience: Releasing control, accepting sacrifice for growth

DEATH
Card number: XIII
Astrological Ruler and Element: Scorpio and Water
Song Inspiration: "Changes"
Symbolism through Song and Keywords: Endings, transformation, rebirth, power
Core Energy: Transformation, endings, deep power
Meaning: Transformation, endings that lead to rebirth, profound change
Reverse Meaning: Resistance to change, fear of endings, stagnation
Soul's Journey: Death of ego/self
Human Experience: Shedding old patterns, embracing deep changes

TEMPERANCE
Card number: XIV
Astrological Ruler and Element: Sagittarius and Fire
Song Inspiration: "One Love"
Symbolism through Song and Keywords: Balance, integration, harmony, alchemy
Core Energy: Expansion, harmony, higher wisdom
Meaning: Harmony, balance, patience, integration, divine timing
Reverse Meaning: Extremes, imbalance, lack of moderation, discord
Soul's Journey: Integration of lessons
Human Experience: Finding inner harmony after chaos

THE DEVIL
Card number: XV
Astrological Ruler and Element: Capricorn and Earth
Song Inspiration: "Toxic"
Symbolism through Song and Keywords: Shadow, addiction, material bondage, ambition, mastery of desire, shadow work, unhealthy attachments
Core Energy: Ambition, mastery, overcoming limitation
Meaning: Shadow self, temptation, materialism, embracing desires
Reverse Meaning: Liberation, breaking free, release of toxic patterns or fears
Soul's Journey: Facing the inner demon
Human Experience: Confronting fear, desire, and unconscious drives

THE TOWER
Card number: XVI
Astrological Ruler and Element: Mars and Fire
Song Inspiration: "The Sound of Silence"
Symbolism through Song and Keywords: Sudden upheaval, revelations, destruction, liberation, war, action, sudden awakening
Core Energy: Destruction, war, action, sudden events
Meaning: Sudden upheaval, revelation, destruction of false foundations
Reverse Meaning: Avoiding necessary change, delayed disaster, fear of collapse
Soul's Journey: The dark night of the soul
Human Experience: Ego shattering, spiritual awakening through destruction

THE STAR
Card number: XVII
Astrological Ruler and Element: Aquarius and Air
Song Inspiration: "Lovely Day"
Symbolism through Song and Keywords: Hope, inspiration, divine guidance, universal connection, universal consciousness
Core Energy: Hope, universal consciousness
Meaning: Hope, renewal, inspiration, spiritual guidance, healing
Reverse Meaning: Despair, loss of faith, hopelessness, lack of vision
Soul's Journey: Receiving the gift
Human Experience: Healing, spiritual renewal, following one's higher calling

THE MOON
Card number: XVIII
Astrological Ruler and Element: Pisces and Water
Song Inspiration: "Thriller"
Symbolism through Song and Keywords: Illusions, intuition, dreams, subconscious, spiritual flow, divine feminine
Core Energy: Illusion, dreams, spiritual surrender
Meaning: Intuition, dreams, mystery, navigating illusion and subconscious.
Reverse Meaning: Fear, confusion, deception, being trapped in illusion.
Soul's Journey: Navigating the subconscious
Human Experience: Discerning truth from illusion, facing fears within

THE SUN
Card number: XIX
Astrological Ruler and Element: Sun and Fire
Song Inspiration: "Happy"
Symbolism through Song and Keywords: Joy, enlightenment, vitality, radiance, life force
Core Energy: Joy, vitality, radiance
Meaning: Joy, vitality, clarity, success, abundance, enlightenment, illumination.
Reverse Meaning: Temporary setbacks, lack of clarity, unrealistic expectations.
Soul's Journey: Ultimate victory
Human Experience: Living authentically. Experiencing clarity and fulfillment

JUDGEMENT
Card number: XX
Astrological Ruler and Element: Pluto and Fire/Water
Song Inspiration: "Wake Up"
Symbolism through Song and Keywords: Awakening, accountability, redemption, rebirth, resurrection, transformation, death
Core Energy: Death, rebirth, transformation
Meaning: Awakening, self-evaluation, redemption, embracing higher calling
Reverse Meaning: Self-doubt, denial, avoidance, ignoring the inner call
Soul's Journey: Return with new wisdom
Human Experience: Answering the higher call, aligning with purpose

THE WORLD
Card number: XXI
Astrological Ruler and Element: Saturn and Earth
Song Inspiration: "We Are The World"
Symbolism through Song and Keywords: Completion, wholeness, harmony, unity, mastery, cycles, worldly achievement, structure
Core Energy: Structure, completion, mastery
Meaning: Completion, mastery, fulfillment, unity, accomplishment
Reverse Meaning: Incompletion, delays, lack of closure, unfinished business.
Soul's Journey: Return to the ordinary world with mastery
Human Experience: Integration of lessons, becoming a whole and conscious being

Minor Arcana

The Minor Arcana represents the day-to-day experiences, challenges, and lessons of human life. While the Major Arcana depicts major spiritual archetypes and life-changing events, the Minor Arcana focuses on the practical, everyday aspects of existence and the actions, emotions, decisions, and relationships that shape our growth over time.

There are 56 Minor Arcana cards, divided into four suits (Wands, Cups, Swords, and Pentacles), each containing 14 cards. The numbered cards Ace through Ten, depict the stages of progress or cycles in that suit's theme. The four court cards (Page, Knight, Queen, and King) represent people, personality traits, or approaches to a situation.

Each suit represents an element and a particular aspect of life. These are like the four elements of experience, showing different ways we interact with the world.

Depending on which framework you use, the suits can also represent alchemy and astrology as well as the aspects of the human being. As it relates to the being, the Wands represent the spiritual, the Cups represent the emotion, the Swords represent the mental (mind and thought), and the Pentacles represent the physical.

Numbered Card Meaning

The numbered cards in each suit show a journey from seed potential (Ace) to completion (Ten). Each number adds a layer of story to the suit that shows how situations evolve from start to finish.

Detailed below is generalized meaning of the numbered cards across the suits.

Number	Meaning
Ace	Beginnings, pure potential, raw energy
Two	Duality, balance, decision-making
Three	Growth, collaboration, initial success
Four	Stability, foundation, security
Five	Conflict, challenge, change
Six	Harmony, restoration, movement forward
Seven	Evaluation, strategy, deeper insight
Eight	Mastery, skill, discipline, transition
Nine	Fulfillment, nearing completion, intensity
Ten	Completion, culmination, end of a cycle

Court Card Meaning

The four court cards in each suit represent people, roles, or energies we embody in different situations. Think of the court cards as a family or a team. The Page gathers ideas. The Knight sets them in motion. The Queen nurtures and refines them. The King leads and brings them to fruition.

Detailed below is generalized meaning of the court cards across the suits.

Court Card	Role	Energy/Personality
Page	The Student, Messenger	Curiosity, learning, exploration
Knight	The Action-Taker, Seeker	Movement, pursuit of goals, passion
Queen	The Nurturer, Teacher	Mastery through compassion, wisdom
King	The Leader, Authority	Mastery through control, vision, maturity

MINOR ARCANA: WANDS

Wands

The Wands touch on the life energies of creativity, passion, career, and spiritual growth. The Wands are tied to the element of fire and symbolizes spirit, passion, and action. The energy is fast-moving, dynamic, and transformative. The Wand challenges are burnout, impulsiveness, and ego-driven. The lessons to learn are to channel energy and use inspiration wisely.

Detailed below is an example of how the flow of energy is viewed through the Wands as it relates to the Zodiac Fire signs:

- Aries (Initiation): Spark of ideas and action.
- Leo (Expression): Passion, leadership, creativity.
- Sagittarius (Expansion): Wisdom, exploration, higher purpose.

Understanding how the energy flows with the elements and the Zodiac signs helps to see how everything is related and inter-related. Therefore, getting a better understanding helps to see the bigger picture to aid in the message and reading.

ACE OF WANDS
Element: Fire *(Pure essence of fire)*
Song Inspiration: "Firework"
Symbolism through Song and Keywords: New beginnings, inspiration, potential
Meaning: Creative spark, exciting, opportunities, motivation, growth
Reverse Meaning: Delays, lack of direction, scattered energy, missed chances

TWO OF WANDS
Astrological Alignment and Element:
Mars in Aries and fire
Song Inspiration: "I've Got The World On A String"
Symbolism through Song and Keywords:
Vision, planning, decisions, holding the future in your hands
Meaning: Future planning, progress, taking steps toward goals
Reverse Meaning: Fear of change, indecision, playing it safe

THREE OF WANDS
Astrological Alignment and Element: Sun in Aries and Fire
Song Inspiration: "Ain't No Mountain High Enough"
Symbolism through Song and Keywords:
Expansion, foresight, exploration beyond limits
Meaning: Growth, opportunities, exploration, success through planning
Reverse Meaning: Obstacles, delays, lack of foresight, unrealistic expectations

FOUR OF WANDS
Astrological Alignment and Element:
Venus in Aries and Fire
Song Inspiration: "Celebration"
Symbolism through Song and Keywords:
Harmony, celebration, stability, milestones, and joyous gatherings
Meaning: Celebration, homecoming, harmony in relationships, success
Reverse Meaning: Tension at home, instability, lack of support

FIVE OF WANDS
Astrological Alignment and Element: Saturn in Leo and Fire
Song Inspiration: "Fight The Power"
Symbolism through Song and Keywords: Conflict, competition, challenge, struggle
Meaning: healthy competition, testing limits, dynamic growth
Reverse Meaning: Hostility, pointless, conflict, unresolved tensions

SIX OF WANDS
Astrological Alignment and Element: Jupiter in Leo and Fire
Song Inspiration: "Eye Of The Tiger"
Symbolism through Song and Keywords: Victory, recognition, pride, triumph
Meaning: Public recognition, success, leadership, progress
Reverse Meaning: Ego-driven pride, lack of acknowledgement, feeling overlooked

SEVEN OF WANDS
Astrological Alignment and Element: Mars in Leo and Fire
Song Inspiration: "Survivor"
Symbolism through Song and Keywords: Defending your position and standing tall, defense, perseverance, courage
Meaning: Standing firm, protecting beliefs, overcoming obstacles
Reverse Meaning: Feeling overwhelmed, burnout, giving up, lack of confidence

EIGHT OF WANDS
Astrological Alignment and Element: Mercury in Sagittarius and Fire
Song Inspiration: "Don't Stop Me Now"
Symbolism through Song and Keywords: Unstoppable momentum, rapid action, progress
Meaning: Swift progress, exciting movement forward, travel, decisive action
Reverse Meaning: Delays, miscommunication, scattered energy, chaos

NINE OF WANDS
Astrological Alignment and Element: Moon in Sagittarius and Fire
Song Inspiration: "Rise Up"
Symbolism through Song and Keywords: Resilience, persistence, strength, endurance after hardship
Meaning: Persistence, inner strength, last stand before success
Reverse Meaning: Exhaustion, paranoia, defensiveness, giving up too soon

TEN OF WANDS
Astrological Alignment and Element: Saturn in Sagittarius and Fire
Song Inspiration: "The Weight"
Symbolism through Song and Keywords: Carrying burdens, responsibility, hard work
Meaning: Completion of a task, responsibility, achievement through effort
Reverse Meaning: Overwhelm, burnout, taking on too much, lack of delegation

PAGE OF WANDS
Element: Fire *(Earth of Fire)*
Song Inspiration: "Start Me Up"
Symbolism through Song and Keywords: Curiosity, exploration, enthusiasm, new adventures, excitement
Meaning: Adventure, creativity, learning, exploring new passions, grounded beginnings
Reverse Meaning: Lack of direction, immaturity, procrastination, self-doubt

KNIGHT OF WANDS
Element: Fire *(Air of Fire)*
Song Inspiration: "Keep On Movin"
Symbolism through Song and Keywords: Action, passion, adventure, boldness, fearless pursuit
Meaning: Courage, excitement, inspired action, fast-moving progress, exploration
Reverse Meaning: Impulsiveness, recklessness, scattered energy

QUEEN OF WANDS
Element: Fire *(Water of Fire)*
Song Inspiration: "Girl On Fire"
**Symbolism through Song and
Keywords:** Charisma, Leadership, influence, inner strength
Meaning: Confidence, emotional warmth, nurturing creativity, independence
Reverse Meaning: Jealously, insecurity, domineering behavior, self-centeredness

KING OF WANDS
Element: Fire *(Fire of Fire)*
Song Inspiration: "Golden"
**Symbolism through Song and
Keywords:** Vision, mastery, leadership
Meaning: Bold leadership, visionary action, inspiring others
Reverse Meaning: Tyranny, arrogance, manipulation, poor planning

MINOR ARCANA: CUPS

Cups

The Cup suit touches on the life energies of emotional foundations, deep transformation, and spiritual transcendence. The Cups are tied to the element of water. The energy is about flow, harmony, and connection. The challenges to overcome are being overwhelmed, emotional imbalance, illusions, and escapism. The lessons to learn are how to balance compassion, intuition, connection, and flow in your life.

Detailed below is an example of how the flow of energy is viewed through the Cups as it relates to the Zodiac Water signs:

- Cancer (Emotional Foundations): Establishing love, trust, family, and connection.

- Scorpio (Deep Transformation): Exploring passion, shadow emotions, intimacy, and hidden truths.

- Pisces (Spiritual Transcendence): Surrendering to universal love, higher guidance, and emotional completion.

ACE OF CUPS
Element: Water *(Pure essence of Water)*
Song Inspiration: "For You"
Symbolism through Song and Keywords: New emotional beginnings, overflowing of love, spiritual flow
Meaning: Emotional awakening, new love, compassion, deep spiritual connection
Reverse Meaning: Emotional blockages, repressed feelings, heartbreak, lost opportunities

TWO OF CUPS
Astrological Alignment and Element:
Venus in Cancer and Water
Song Inspiration: "Always And Forever"
Symbolism through Song and Keywords:
Unity, connection, romantic harmony, partnership
Meaning: Mutual attraction, harmonious union, balanced relationships
Reverse Meaning: Disharmony, imbalance, separation, misunderstandings

THREE OF CUPS
Astrological Alignment and Element:
Mercury in Cancer and Water
Song Inspiration: "We Are Family"
Symbolism through Song and Keywords:
Celebration, friendship, community, joyful connection
Meaning: Joy, friendship, celebrations, emotional support networks
Reverse Meaning: Gossip, overindulgence, broken trust, isolation

FOUR OF CUPS
Astrological Alignment and Element:
Moon in Cancer and Water
Song Inspiration: "I Still Haven't Found What I'm Looking For"
Symbolism through Song and Keywords:
Longing, dissatisfaction, and emotional contemplation, re-evaluation, apathy
Meaning: Inner-reflection, re-assessing options, seeking deeper meaning
Reverse Meaning: Stagnation, missed opportunities, emotional disconnection

FIVE OF CUPS
Astrological Alignment and Element: Mars in Scorpio and Water
Song Inspiration: "Un-Break My Heart"
Symbolism through Song and Keywords: Loss, grief, disappointment, emotional pain
Meaning: Mourning, emotional pain, focusing on what's lost
Reverse Meaning: Acceptance, forgiveness, moving forward, finding hope

SIX OF CUPS
Astrological Alignment and Element: Sun in Scorpio and Water
Song Inspiration: "Remember The Time"
Symbolism through Song and Keywords: Nostalgia, innocence, healing, memories, reconnection with the past
Meaning: Childhood memories, reconciliation, kindness, healing the past
Reverse Meaning: Being stuck in the past, unrealistic ideas, clinging to old wounds

SEVEN OF CUPS
Astrological Alignment and Element: Venus in Scorpio and Water
Song Inspiration: "Boulevard Of Broken Dreams"
Symbolism through Song and Keywords: Choices, illusion, fantasy, emotional confusion
Meaning: Opportunities, dreams, imagination, spiritual exploration
Reverse Meaning: Confusion, illusion, temptation, lack of clarity

EIGHT OF CUPS
Astrological Alignment and Element:
Saturn in Pisces and Water
Song Inspiration: "I Will Always Love You"
Symbolism through Song and Keywords:
Walking away and letting go, but with love and grace. Transition, spiritual journey
Meaning: Walking away, soul searching, leaving behind what no longer serves you
Reverse Meaning: Fear of change, stagnation, avoidance of deeper truths

NINE OF CUPS
Astrological Alignment and Element:
Jupiter in Pisces and Water
Song Inspiration: "Good As Hell"
Symbolism through Song and Keywords:
Emotional fulfillment and self-love. Satisfaction, emotional abundance
Meaning: Fulfilment, happiness, emotional harmony, wish fulfillment
Reverse Meaning: Dissatisfaction, indulgence, arrogance, fleeting happiness

TEN OF CUPS
Astrological Alignment and Element:
Mars in Pisces and Water
Song Inspiration: "Happy Together"
Symbolism through Song and Keywords:
Harmony, family, shared emotional joy
Meaning: Lasting happiness, emotional harmony, joy, and love
Reverse Meaning: Broken relationships, instability, disharmony, unrealistic expectations

PAGE OF CUPS
Element: Water *(Earth of Water)*
Song Inspiration: "Just The Two Of Us"
Symbolism through Song and Keywords: Playful emotional exploration, innocence, creativity, intuition
Meaning: Intuitive, messages, emotional beginnings, new creative ventures
Reverse Meaning: Emotional immaturity, insecurity, escapism, emotional blocks

KNIGHT OF CUPS
Element: Water *(Air of Water)*
Song Inspiration: "Let's Get It On"
Symbolism through Song and Keywords: Romance, pursuit of dreams and passions
Meaning: Idealism, romance, following one's heart, inspired action
Reverse Meaning: Unrealistic expectations, moodiness, manipulation, over sensitivity

QUEEN OF CUPS
Element: Water *(Water of Water)*
Song Inspiration: "Vision Of Love"
Symbolism through Song and Keywords: Compassion, empathy, nurturing, emotional wisdom
Meaning: Deep emotional wisdom, unconditional love, psychic abilities
Reverse Meaning: Overwhelm, co-dependency, emotional manipulation, lack of boundaries

KING OF CUPS
Element: Water *(Fire of Water)*
Song Inspiration: "Lean On Me"
Symbolism through Song and Keywords: Emotional mastery, compassionate leadership
Meaning: Emotional maturity, diplomacy, harmony, compassion with strength
Reverse Meaning: Repression, emotional imbalance, coldness, controlling behaviors

MINOR ARCANA: SWORDS

Swords

The Swords suit touches on the life energies of thought, communication, power of words, decisions, conflict, and truth. The Swords are tied to the element of air. The energy is about the mental realm, showing how thoughts and communication shape reality. The challenges to overcome are confusion, deception, cruelty, and mental stress. The lessons to learn are how to positively express clarity, fairness, intellect, and breakthroughs of understanding.

Detailed below is an example of how the flow of energy is viewed through the Swords as it relates to the Zodiac Air signs:

- Libra (Balance & Relationships): Mental conflict, choices, and harmony versus discord.

- Aquarius (Innovation & Strategy): Social dynamics, deception, and intellectual challenges.

- Gemini (Thought & Communication): Overwhelm, anxiety, and eventual release or clarity.

ACE OF SWORDS
Element: Air *(Pure essence of Air)*
Song Inspiration: "A Change Is Gonna Come"
Symbolism through Song and Keywords: Clarity, truth, new ideas, insight
Meaning: Breakthrough, mental clarity, fresh perspectives, decisive action
Reverse Meaning: Confusion, clouded judgment, lies, missed opportunities

TWO OF SWORDS
Astrological Alignment and Element: Moon in Libra and Air
Song Inspiration: "Should I Stay Or Should I Go"
Symbolism through Song and Keywords: Balance, decisions, duality
Meaning: Stalemate, difficult choices, inner conflict, finding equilibrium
Reverse Meaning: Indecision, confusion, avoidance, hidden truths revealed

THREE OF SWORDS
Astrological Alignment and Element: Saturn in Libra and Air
Song Inspiration: "Tears Dry On Their Own"
Symbolism through Song and Keywords: Heartbreak, grief, separation, sorry
Meaning: Emotional pain, loss, betrayal, heartbreak
Reverse Meaning: Forgiveness, recovery, releasing pain, reconciliation

FOUR OF SWORDS
Astrological Alignment and Element: Jupiter in Libra and Air
Song Inspiration: "Let's Chill"
Symbolism through Song and Keywords: Rest, recovery after conflict, reflection
Meaning: Healing, rest, meditation, preparation for renewal
Reverse Meaning: Burnout, stress, inability to rest, mental overload

FIVE OF SWORDS
Astrological Alignment and Element: Venus in Aquarius and Air
Song Inspiration: "Backstabbers"
Symbolism through Song and Keywords: Conflict, tension, discord, betrayal, hollow victory
Meaning: Disputes, competition, hollow victory, ego battles
Reverse Meaning: Resolution, reconciliation, lessons learned, moving on

SIX OF SWORDS
Astrological Alignment and Element: Mercury in Aquarius and Air
Song Inspiration: "Bridge Over Troubled Water"
Symbolism through Song and Keywords: Transition, movement, progress, healing
Meaning: Moving on, healing journey, leaving difficulties behind
Reverse Meaning: Emotional baggage, resisting change, lack of closure

SEVEN OF SWORDS
Astrological Alignment and Element: Moon in Aquarius and Air
Song Inspiration: "Smooth Criminal"
Symbolism through Song and Keywords: Strategy, secrecy, deception, cunning
Meaning: Cleverness, strategic planning, adaptability, secrecy
Reverse Meaning: Betrayal, being caught, self-deception, running from truth

EIGHT OF SWORDS
Astrological Alignment and Element: Jupiter in Gemini and Air
Song Inspiration: "Trapped"
Symbolism through Song and Keywords: Feeling imprisoned by thoughts or circumstances. Restriction, limitation, fear
Meaning: Feeling trapped, mental blockages, self-imposed limits
Reverse Meaning: Liberation, gaining clarity, breaking free, empowerment

NINE OF SWORDS
Astrological Alignment and Element: Mars in Gemini and Air
Song Inspiration: "Every Breath You Take"
Symbolism through Song and Keywords: Anxiety, despair, paranoia, inner torment, nightmares
Meaning: Worry, guilt, insomnia, fear, mental anguish
Reverse Meaning: Healing, release of worry, facing fears, hope returns

TEN OF SWORDS
Astrological Alignment and Element: Sun in Gemini and Air
Song Inspiration: "Hurt"
Symbolism through Song and Keywords: Painful endings, deep sorrow, betrayal, collapse
Meaning: Final ending, destruction, painful completion
Reverse Meaning: Recovery, regeneration, hope after devastation

PAGE OF SWORDS
Element: Air *(Earth of Air)*
Song Inspiration: "Talk"
Symbolism through Song and Keywords: Curiosity, exploration, seeking truth, intellect
Meaning: New ideas, learning, vigilance, curiosity
Reverse Meaning: Gossip, deception, miscommunication, lack of focus

KNIGHT OF SWORDS
Element: Air *(Air of Air)*
Song Inspiration: "Run This Town"
Symbolism through Song and Keywords: Action, speed, ambition
Meaning: Bold action, pursuit of goals, fast-moving change
Reverse Meaning: Recklessness, impulsiveness, scattered energy, arrogance

QUEEN OF SWORDS
Element: Air *(Water of Air)*
Song Inspiration: "Irreplaceable"
Symbolism through Song and Keywords: Wisdom, truth, clarity, independence, strong boundaries
Meaning: Clear thinking, honesty, discernment, intellectual strength
Reverse Meaning: Coldness, bitterness, manipulation, overly critical

KING OF SWORDS
Element: Air *(Fire of Air)*
Song Inspiration: "Masterpiece"
Symbolism through Song and Keywords: Authority, mastery, justice, wise decision-making
Meaning: Intellectual power, truth, balanced decisions, leadership
Reverse Meaning: Corruption, tyranny, misuse of power, lack of clarity

MINOR ARCANA: PENTACLES

Pentacles

The Pentacles suit touches on the life energies of finances, health, career, home, and physical well-being. The Pentacles are tied to the element of Earth. The energy represents the material world, including work, finances, home, health, security, grounding, and physical manifestation. The challenges to overcome are greed, stagnation, over-attachment, and materialism. The lessons to learn are how to positively express stability, abundance, nurturing growth, and manifestation.

Detailed below is an example of how the flow of energy is viewed through the Pentacles as it relates to the Zodiac Earth signs:

- Capricorn (Structure and Building): Planning foundations, discipline, and ambition.
- Taurus (Value and Stability): Security, comfort, patience, and resource management.
- Virgo (Refinement and Mastery): Skill development, efficiency, and service to others.

ACE OF PENTACLES
Element: Earth *(Pure essence of Earth)*
Song Inspiration: "Money (That's What I Want)"
Symbolism through Song and Keywords: The seed of prosperity and new material opportunities, abundance, manifestation
Meaning: New financial or career opportunities, prosperity, solid beginnings
Reverse Meaning: Missed chances, instability, lack of planning, financial mismanagement

TWO OF PENTACLES
Astrological Alignment and Element: Jupiter in Capricorn and Earth
Song Inspiration: "Workin Day And Night"
Symbolism through Song and Keywords: Balancing responsibilities and juggling priorities, adaptability, resource management
Meaning: Time management, balancing priorities, flexibility, harmony amid change
Reverse Meaning: Overwhelm, imbalance, disorganization, lack of focus

THREE OF PENTACLES
Astrological Alignment and Element: Mars in Capricorn and Earth
Song Inspiration: "I'll Be There For You"
Symbolism through Song and Keywords: Collaboration, teamwork, skill, skill-building
Meaning: Mastery through collaboration, recognition for work, cooperation
Reverse Meaning: Lack of teamwork, poor planning, disharmony, unrecognized efforts

FOUR OF PENTACLES
Astrological Alignment and Element: Sun in Capricorn and Earth
Song Inspiration: "She's Working Hard For The Money"
Symbolism through Song and Keywords: Holding tightly to resources, stability, control, or security
Meaning: Financial security, saving resources, stability, protecting assets
Reverse Meaning: Greed, possessiveness, fear of loss, unhealthy attachments

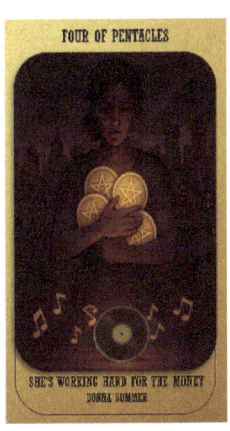

FIVE OF PENTACLES
Astrological Alignment and Element: Mercury in Taurus and Earth
Song Inspiration: "Stormy Weather"
Symbolism through Song and Keywords: Hardship, struggle, loss, seeking support
Meaning: Financial loss, health struggles, feeling left out, lack of support
Reverse Meaning: Recovery, new opportunities, improving health or finances

SIX OF PENTACLES
Astrological Alignment and Element: Moon in Taurus and Earth
Song Inspiration: "True Colors"
Symbolism through Song and Keywords: Generosity, balance, giving and receiving
Meaning: Charity, generosity, financial help, fairness, harmony in exchanges
Reverse Meaning: Strings attached, inequality, exploitation, selfishness

SEVEN OF PENTACLES
Astrological Alignment and Element: Saturn in Taurus and Earth
Song Inspiration: "Patience"
Symbolism through Song and Keywords: Long-term growth, waiting, and reflection. Patience, assessment, perseverance
Meaning: Long-term planning, investment, waiting for results, steady progress
Reverse Meaning: Impatience, wasted effort, poor planning, lack of vision

EIGHT OF PENTACLES
Astrological Alignment and Element: Sun in Virgo and Earth
Song Inspiration: "Taking Care of Business"
Symbolism through Song and Keywords: Mastery through consistent effort and skill-building. Skill, mastery, diligence
Meaning: Hard work, dedication, learning new skills, craftsmanship
Reverse Meaning: Perfectionism, burnout, lack of focus, work dissatisfaction

NINE OF PENTACLES
Astrological Alignment and Element: Venus in Virgo and Earth
Song Inspiration: "Independent Women"
Symbolism through Song and Keywords: Independence, luxury, self-sufficiency, enjoying the fruits of labor
Meaning: Financial independence, self-reliance, abundance, refinement
Reverse Meaning: Overindulgence, dependency, superficiality, reckless spending

TEN OF PENTACLES
Astrological Alignment and Element: Mercury in Virgo and Earth
Song Inspiration: "Family Affair"
Symbolism through Song and Keywords: Legacy, family, stability
Meaning: Financial security, family heritage, long-term success, generational wealth
Reverse Meaning: Family conflict, instability, poor investments, fleeting wealth

PAGE OF PENTACLES
Element: Earth *(Earth of Earth)*
Song Inspiration: "Dream On"
Symbolism through Song and Keywords: Ambition and the beginning of a material journey. Curiosity, study, grounded beginnings
Meaning: Learning, new financial opportunities, practical skills, planning
Reverse Meaning: Lack of focus, procrastination, missed chances, short-sightedness

KNIGHT OF PENTACLES
Element: Earth *(Air of Earth)*
Song Inspiration: "Hard Workin' Man"
Symbolism through Song and Keywords: Routine, responsibility, persistence
Meaning: Hard work, reliability, steady progress, dedication
Reverse Meaning: Stagnation, laziness, workaholism, lack of ambition

QUEEN OF PENTACLES
Element: Earth *(Water of Earth)*
Song Inspiration: "Superwoman"
Symbolism through Song and Keywords:
Nurturing abundance and balancing care with practicality
Meaning: Caregiving, creating security, balancing home and work, generosity
Reverse Meaning: Overwhelm, imbalance, neglect, over-dependence

KING OF PENTACLES
Element: Earth *(Fire of Earth)*
Song Inspiration: "For The Love Of Money"
Symbolism through Song and Keywords:
Mastery of wealth and leadership with responsibility. Leadership, mastery, prosperity
Meaning: Financial mastery, success, generosity, responsible leadership
Reverse Meaning: Greed, corruption, financial failure, materialism

Type of Card Spreads and When to Use Them

There are many classic types of card spreads to use as starters when reading. Some spreads are better than others when clarifying questions and energies.

Detailed below is a guiding list of when to use certain spreads and the purpose of a particular spread. This is not an exhaustive list. As you become more familiar and comfortable with your cards, you'll begin to learn more spreads and adapt your spreads based on the questions and situations.

Choosing the Right Spread

The spread you use determines how the cards are interpreted and how their positions tell a story. Each spread provides a structure for exploring different aspects of a question, situation, or spiritual journey.

Need	Recommended Spread
Quick guidance	Daily draw or Three-card
Relationships	Two-card, Three-card, or Relationship spread
Career / Decisions	Cross of clarity, Horseshoe, Career path spread
Spiritual growth	Chakra spread, Shadow work spread
Full life overview	Celtic Cross, 9-Box Life Map

Common Single, Two, and Three Card Spreads

The following are common types of tarot spreads, organized by complexity and purpose, along with what they're best used for.

Spread Type	Spread Name	Purpose	When to Use
Single card	Daily draw	A message or theme for the day	Daily guidance, mediation focus
Single card	Yes / No Insight	Quick clarity with interpretation leaning positive or negative	Fast decisions, simple questions
Single card	Card of the Year	Overarching theme for a month or year	Annual readings, New Year rituals
Two-card	Choice Spread	Compare two paths or decisions	1. Option A 2. Option B
Two-card	Problem / Solution	Identify issue and possible resolution	1. Problem 2. Solution
Two-card	You / Other Person	Examine relationship dynamics	1. You 2. Them
Three-card	Past / Present / Future	1. Past 2. Present 3. Future	Timeline view of a situation
Three-card	Mind / Body / Spirit	1. Mind 2. Body 3. Spirit	Holistic self-awareness
Three-card	Situation / Action / Outcome	1. Current situation 2. Advice or action 3. Likely outcome	Problem-solving

Common Three, Four, and Five Card Spreads

Spread Type	Spread Name	Purpose	When to Use
Three-card	You / Relationship/ Partner	1. You 2. Relationship energy 3. Partner	Relationship readings
Three-card	Obstacle /Tool/ Lesson	1. Challenge 2. Resource 3. Wisdom gained	Spiritual growth
Four-card	Four Elements Spread	1. Fire (Spirit, willpower) 2. Water (Emotions) 3. Air (Thoughts) 4. Earth (Material world)	Balanced life assessment
Four-card	Four Corners Spread	1. Strengths 2. Weaknesses 3. Opportunities 4. Threats	SWOT-style reading
Four-card	Seasonal Spread	1. Spring (Growth) 2. Summer (Fruition) 3. Fall (Release) 4. Winter (Rest)	Clarifying cycles or yearly patterns
Five-card	Cross of Clarity	1. Situation 2. Challenge 3. Hidden factor 4. Advice 5. Outcome	Overview of a situation
Five-card	Elemental Flow	1. Fire (action) 2. Water (emotion) 3. Air (thought) 4. Earth (manifestation) 5. Spirit (overall)	Spiritual alignment

Common Five, Seven, and Nine Card Spreads

Spread Type	Spread Name	Purpose	When to Use
Five-card	Past / Present / Future with Insight	1. Past 2. Present 3. Future 4. Challenge 5. Guidance	Adds complexity to a timeline reading
Seven-card	Horseshoe Spread	Past, Present, Hidden Influences, Obstacles, External Influences, Suggested Action, Outcome	Insight into external factors and choices
Seven-card	Chakra Spread	Root, Sacral, Solar Plexus, Heart, Throat, Third Eye, Crown	Energy alignment and blockages
Seven-card	Weekly Forecast	Day-by-day for seven days	Planning and weekly guidance
Nine-card	9-box life map	3x3 grid	1. Mind 2. Heart 3. Body 4. Work 5. Home 6. Spirit 7. Challenges 8. Strengths 9. Outcome

Celtic Cross Spread (Classic and Comprehensive)

The Celtic Cross is one of the most well-known tarot spreads, offering deep, multi-faceted insight. It can also be used for comprehensive readings covering past, present, and future.

Position	Meaning
1. The Present	Current situation or issue
2. The Challenge	Obstacle or opposing force
3. The Foundation	Root cause or underlying influence
4. The Past	Energy or events fading away
5. The Goal	Desired outcome or focus
6. The Future	Next step or near-future influence
7. The Self	The querent's perspective or state of mind
8. External Influences	People or forces impacting the situation
9. Hopes & Fears	Internal hopes and fears shaping choices
10. Outcome	Probable result if current path continues

Position of Classic Celtic Cross Spread

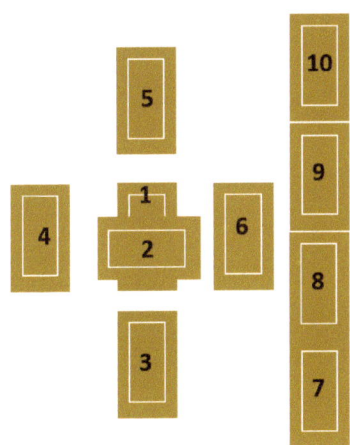

Specialty and Spiritual Spreads

The list of spreads below are best used for focused, specific life areas, or deep inner work readings and guidance.

Spread Name	Purpose	Example Use
Relationship Spread	Explore romantic or relational dynamics	You, Partner, Relationship energy, Challenges, Advice, Outcome
Career Path Spread	Identify career direction and obstacles	Current position, Goals, Strengths, Obstacles, Advice, Potential
Shadow Work Spread	Deep healing and self-awareness	Shadow self, Root cause, Impact, Integration, Higher self-guidance
Spiritual Growth Spread	Track spiritual awakening stages	Past self, Present self, Challenges, Guidance, Spiritual purpose

Interpreting Timing in Tarot

One of the most intriguing challenges for any tarot reader is learning how to interpret when an event might unfold. Unlike clocks or calendars, the tarot speaks the language of energy, alignment, and momentum. Timing in tarot is not fixed, it reflects how ready a situation or individual is to move forward. The cards reveal the rhythm of unfolding events rather than an exact date on the calendar. When you draw a card, you are not seeing a deadline but an energetic pattern showing the pace and readiness of transformation.

Each suit offers clues about the tempo of manifestation. Wands, born of fire, move swiftly. This is often a signaling that change or inspiration is already in motion and may arrive within days or weeks. Swords, ruled by air, bring quick but mental progress, suggesting developments that unfold over several weeks or through decisions and conversations. Cups, aligned with water, flow more slowly. They mirror emotional growth, relationships, and healing processes that take time to mature, often across months or seasonal shifts. Pentacles, the steady earth element, mark the slowest movement of all, indicating growth, construction, and tangible results that may take months or even years to fully materialize. By observing the element present, you can sense whether a situation is taking root, building momentum, or already igniting.

Astrology deepens this temporal understanding. Many cards, especially the Major Arcana, align with zodiac signs and planetary influences that correspond to specific seasons or time frames. For example, The Emperor resonates with Aries, representing the spring equinox and the spark of initiation, while The Hermit, tied to Virgo, speaks to the reflective period of late summer. In readings, these astrological clues may reveal when the energy will be most active or when the intentions of the one questioning will align with cosmic cycles.

Numbers also whisper their own sense of rhythm. Aces herald immediacy and beginnings, the first step of potential. Twos introduce decisions and duality, a pause before commitment. Threes open expansion and visible growth. Tens bring closure, signaling the end of one phase and preparation for the next. Reading numerological progression helps gauge how far along the questioner stands within their cycle and whether the outcome is imminent or still waiting to come forth.

Ultimately, tarot timing is energetic, not mechanical. To read timing of events through tarot is to sense how the invisible currents of energy move through life's seasons. Timing in tarot is not prediction but participation. It's the art of sensing when the spirit and the world are ready to meet.

Reading The Cards

Using the 3-Card Spread

The 3-card spread is a very simple spread. Just remember to be clear on your purpose and what you are clarifying. For the example, we are going to use the past, present, and future as the purpose. It also needs to be clear when you are doing any spread, which card you intend to pull first and its position. I clarify this point, because as you become in tune with the energy, you become in tune with your tools. Therefore, your intentions need to be clear.

Past	Present	Future

Using the 7-Card Spread

For the 7-card spread example, let's use the 7 chakras as the purpose to see where the alignments and blockages are. This spread is good to help to understand spiritual growth.

Root   Sacral   Solar Plexus   Heart   Throat   3rd Eye   Crown

Tips for Effective Readings

- The clearer the question, the more focused the reading.
- Define each card's position before drawing.
- Even with a structured spread, trust your intuition to connect patterns.
- Modify spreads to fit unique situations or your personal style.
- Have fun.

Author's Note

Creating the *Energy in Song Tarot* has been a learning experience, an act of love, rhythm, and remembrance. Each card was born from the understanding that music and spirit speak the same language. The songs that inspired this deck echo the same truths found in the tarot. The songs invoke lessons of love, loss, power, and transformation. Just as every song carries a story, so too does every card.

This guidebook is my invitation for you to slow down, listen, and feel the energy around you. Let the melodies of the cards move through you like a favorite track that always seems to play at the right time. Whether you're seeking clarity, healing, or inspiration, may these cards remind you that your soul has its own rhythm and that rhythm will always guide you home.

ENERGY IN SONG

TAROT

Guidebook

MAY THE SPARK OF INSPIRATION ILLUMINATE YOUR PATH

MAY THE DIVINE GUIDE YOUR STEPS

MAY YOUR THOUGHTS BE IN ALIGNMENT WITH YOUR TRUTH

MAY YOU MANIFEST YOUR DREAMS

www.ingramcontent.com/pod-product-compliance
Lightning Source LLC
Chambersburg PA
CBHW041626220426
43663CB00001B/29